Sophia

I'm Back!

You're not alone! Rise above *that* circumstance and be free from the past. All it takes is the desire to succeed and the will to push ahead. Learn how one girl rose above her past to become a dreamer and sexual abuse survivor.

The True Story of Sophia Antwonique Strother

Sophia

Printed in the United States of America.

All scriptures used are from BibleGateway.com © Copyright 1995-2008. All rights reserved.

ISBN 10: 1-4528-4690-1
ISBN 13: 978-1-4528-4690-3

Trustworthy Consulting
Empowerment Driven by Knowledge Coalition
P.O. Box 273
Waco, Texas 76703
www.trustworthyconsult.com
trustworthy.consulting@yahoo.com
(254) 495-5556 direct

Front Cover Design by: Transgraphics Inc.
Back Cover Design by: Jamal Gillis
Cover & Interior Photo by: Shante Tasby
Edited by: Linda Crawford, The Anchor News, Waco

This book is an honest and accurate account of my life, journey and spiritual encounter with God insofar as I can remember and recount based upon study of the Word and personal experience. The first names of a few individuals have been altered to protect their identities however the incidents and experiences have not.

First Edition.

I'm Back!

Sophia

DEDICATION

Jesus ~ *I owe my whole existence and purpose to your death and resurrection. Thank you for your journey and sufferings that has allowed me to experience the joys of life and expectation of Heaven.*

My children Zavier, Dondre' and Le'loni~ *the true loves of my life. I never thought I could fully give my heart and soul to anyone but all of you managed to penetrate my being and grab my heart. All that I do is for you and God. I pray that you never succumb to your circumstances and know that mom made it and so can you.*

Aunt Sonia ~ *I love you so much and thank God that you took your rightful place as my "Mom" when my biological mother couldn't handle it. You've been so good to my family and me. There's nothing I could say or do to show my most intimate appreciation and lifelong bond that you've created. I pray you will be swept off your feet by your prince charming and reap all of the great seeds you've planted in my life.*

Oprah Winfrey ~ *I plan on meeting you one day to personally thank you for being an inspiration to me by just having victory over your past. You've showed me despite my childhood I can overcome it and be successful in all that I do and dream. It's not about the financial wealth; it's about the spiritual, personal and family wealth that makes us successful in life.*

Sophia

TABLE OF CONTENTS

I'm Back!

Sophia

Mother, mother where art thou?

That name... God

Road of Life

Dad, is that you?

My journey from the Grave

Today, I leave the cemetery. Today I live!

Reality Check

Statistics

You can do it!

I'm Back!

Sophia

FORWARD

I'm Back!

Sophia

CROSSOVER FROM VICTIM OF LIFE TO SURVIVOR
Learn about one girl's journey of survival and then start your own!

In 1989, a father molested his little girl. She was nine years old. This molestation would continue for the next two years. Additionally, this child would be raped three times by three other men. Each violation would take more and more of her identity and self-worth.

In her self-titled book, *Sophia ~ I'm Back*, she says, "By the age of sixteen, I felt like a washed up rag. I felt like – what else!" BUT there was an underlying strength that God had given her to overcome the unimaginable: having parents who were on drugs, being homeless and being pregnant at 15 years old. With a strength that comes only from God, she had a shear determination to defy the odds and stereotypes to become a SURVIVOR and Champion for Success.

After watching a documentary on Oprah Winfrey, she realized they had similar pasts. At that moment she said, "If Oprah can decide not to allow her past to dictate her future, then I refuse to be another statistic." From then on,

I'm Back! 7

Sophia

Sophia was propelled into her true destiny…being an inspiration and role model for other women and children to follow.

Her critically acclaimed book, *Sophia ~ I'm Back,* is filled with remedies for past hurts, disappointments, abuse, loneliness and guilt. It tackles many of the myths surrounding sexual abuse and provides the FACTS that

every parent and person should know. From the 2005 hit Paramount movie *Coach Carter* starring Samuel L. Jackson, the real Coach Ken Carter motivated Sophia to shout her story from the mountaintops. Since then, she has been traveling all over the US bringing a new found joy, self-esteem and empowerment to victims of sexual abuse and just plain life.

Those who feel as if their past or current circumstances have kept them bound will find this woman's journey a true inspiration for all ages, genders and demographics. As she so elegantly states in her speeches and travels all over the United States, *"The sky is NOT the limit,"* Sophia A Strother has dedicated her life to empowering others to live, love and laugh.

I'm Back!

Sophia

She is currently working alongside Martin Luther King III and his organization, Realizing the Dream, in bringing hope to East Waco and Marlin, Texas. Sophia is also working closely with Coach Carter and his foundation in spreading the message on the importance of education as the priority in our youth's future. Last, she has recently partnered with LaDainian Tomlinson, formerly #21 with the San Diego Chargers (RB), and his mother in hosting "A Time for Change" Symposium and Investors Brunch. Trying to save his hometown, Marlin, Texas, LaDainian is striving to raise awareness on the importance of economic development.

Sophia

Philippians 1:12-13 (NIV)

Now I want you to know, brothers, that what has happened to me has really served to advance the gospel. As a result, it has become clear throughout the whole palace guard and to everyone else that I am in chains for Christ.

Dear Friends,

This scripture reveals exactly how I feel about my journey thus far. I've gone through so much so God can get the glory. My desire is that my testimony will encourage people who're going through to know that they can make it, that they're not alone and that God will never leave nor forsake them. I'll never forget the saying, "God's Will, will never take you where God's Grace can't protect you." Remember, He's always there!

Sophia A. Strother

I'm Back!

Sophia

REFLECTION AFTER THE

STORM

Sophia

W ho would've thought that by the age of 29 I would have gone through so much and survived? How I survived could only be accredited to the Man Upstairs. I used to say "Why have I had to endure such a turbulent life all before the age of sixteen"; but now as I begin to age and gain wisdom spiritually, I realize that this journey of life has just been a stepping stone to what God truly has for my family and me. I can remember many times that I cried and prayed to feel my age for just one day. Not a lifetime but one day. Asking the question, "When can I feel normal, appreciated and loved? Why, can't I stop

I'm Back!

making the stupid mistakes I know are demeaning me as a woman, as a mother and as a person? Will I ever find someone that truly loves me for me and not what I have to offer sexually?" This is my life. I'm telling you true thoughts and feelings. After being deceived your whole childhood with molestation, rape, emotional abuse and parents that succumbed to drugs you ask the question "WHY." I didn't ask for this life I was born into it and I just want to know "WHY." After a while I stop asking why and started saying "YES" to God. Whatever your will,

Sophia

whatever you have for me to do, wherever you want me to go, just let me know. This is a journey of a little girl, a young lady and woman who defied the stereotypes and the odds to become a dreamer and a survivor for other women who are experiencing the storm or drying off from the rain.

Sophia

~ CROOKED ROOTS ~

HOW ARE YOURS

GROWING?

I'm Back!

Sophia

Train up the child and when he is old he will not depart....Proverbs 22:6

But what if you don't train them up?

I grew up in a shroud of mystery and deceit. The furthest I can go back is our first home on Union Street in Springfield, Massachusetts. It was a small yet comfortable two story yellow home. The front yard had a wire fence snuggly wrapped around it. In the back, the two car garage was on its last limb

I'm Back!

with an amputated basketball hoop in the middle. My parents were successful in building a deck onto the back of the house large enough to house our award winning grill that my father so affectionately cuddled all through the summer. Inside the front door immediately revealed steps leading upstairs and a modest living room set on the left. The shot-gun like design pointed straight through to the kitchen, dining room and door leading to the backyard on the right. My parents' room was at the top of the stairs, our doorless bathroom to the far right and my room was right next to my parents in the middle. I was

Sophia

born at that house in 1980 and left when I was about 6 years old.

I still remember my father working at Baystate Gas Company coming home every evening in his dark blue overalls and scuffed black boots. He would run through the front door, give me a huge bear hug and exclaim, "I'm home sweetheart!" I used to anticipate those words daily. It was like having a daily fix of sugar; everything was sweet and lovely. Every morning he'd wake me up with "Time to rise and shine." These words are forever etched into my mind. He loved to make bacon and eggs, and even though every morning the

I'm Back!

bacon was burnt, I ate them as if they were the best thing since sliced bread. My dad had no rhythm, bless his heart. He would turn on the 8 track—yes I was born when 8 tracks and records were still in—and dance around like he was doing the Hokey Pokey; however, he got stuck at turning himself around. I remember going to the race track at Riverside Park, now Six Flags in Agawam, Massachusetts. Watching the car races, I was always so excited that I was with my dad.

I really don't remember much about my mother. I don't know where she worked or what she did during the day. She really didn't

Sophia

have set routines with me. Our home on Union Street was passed down through two generations. My father's mother's family grew up in this house, and then they passed it onto her, my nana Vivienne Ernestine Strother Adams. After she bought a home on Cedar Street, she then passed the home on to my father. I have to admit my life at this point seemed flawless. I went to the Boys and Girls Club and summer camp regularly. I had a home in a decent neighborhood and parents who never argued (at least not in front of me), and I was an only child, but when I was six, things started to change.

I'm Back!

Sophia

We moved to Sixteen Acres around 1986 into our first really nice home to live out the "Jefferson" dream. We jubilantly sang, *We're movin' on up*. However, once there I remember feeling lost and alone. All of my friends now stayed far away, and we rarely went back to visit. Our new neighborhood was dressed with nice moderate homes. Most had two parents, two cars and maybe a mobile home to travel with. I was one of the few African American children in the neighborhood. Even though children tend not to care about those things when they are younger, I noticed. My mother started to travel

Sophia

to nice remote places with her girlfriend, Kim. One year she went to Hawaii and the next Acapulco, Mexico. My father and I never went with her. My father was still working for Baystate Gas Company. I would slowly but surely start seeing my life break into a million piece puzzle—one that would take me more than fifteen years to put back together.

We didn't go to church, but my parents lived honest lives. I thought. They had very good careers, a nice home and stayed to themselves. Everything came to a halting end when I was nine years old. We moved from Sixteen Acres out of a beautiful home

I'm Back!

after my father had a seizure. To this day I
don't know why he had a seizure however
when we left I felt like belting out, "So, we're
moving on down!" I didn't know why we were
moving. I just knew we were leaving the
"Jefferson" dream. Moving to West
Springfield, Massachusetts about 1988 or
1989, we crammed our belongings into a two-
bedroom apartment off Riverdale Road. Dad
and I were home alone like usual, (because
my mother was normally gone in the evenings
for her job) and we were watching TV on the
floor in the living room of our two bedroom
apartment. I noticed dad was dosing off, but I

wasn't tired so I continued to lie on my stomach resting my face on my hands. Suddenly my dad turned on his side and slid his hands in my pants and starting playing with my behind, then moved to my vagina. I didn't move. I lay there, holding my breath, not knowing what to do or think. I knew this didn't feel right or natural. I remember thinking to myself, "Maybe he's dreaming and thinks I am my Mom." He continued to fondle me for awhile and then abruptly stopped. No words were spoken and no eye contact exchanged. I couldn't move; I couldn't even breathe; I lay there quietly, confused. I didn't

I'm Back!

know what to think, and I didn't know what it meant. I remember just laying there. I just didn't know.

It's amazing how eighteen years later as I'm recounting the death of my innocence, I cry. When you're young, you don't deal with your emotions because you don't realize exactly what you're feeling. You rebel, react and fight what's going on inside and what's happening around you. That was the first of many inappropriate interactions between my dad and me—interactions that lasted for two years.

Sophia

These encounters with my father definitely followed me into my relationships. With an abused

child, normally, the predators try to develop the fear of death into the child's mind. Often, they say things like, "If you tell anybody I'll hurt you" (or someone the child loves), or "Nobody will believe you if you tell," or "You're a nobody" or "I'm doing this for your own good." I always went with the flow when it came to men, especially in the case of being naive. I would stay in a dysfunctional relationship; afraid to voice my objections for fear that perhaps I had caused him to act this way.

I'm Back!

Sophia

"Maybe it is not him," I said to myself over and over. "If I say something, he might get mad at me," I would think.

I would often settle for drama or neglect my feelings. I would think, "Maybe he'll come around," or the worst theory, "I can change him." Oh ladies, we need to leave those feelings and thoughts buried. It's never your fault when you're physically, mentally or sexually abused. And the most important thought to leave buried is thinking you can change a person that is an abuser. It's not our job to be their punching bags or sexual relief doll.

Sophia

The majority of the sexual degradation that my father subjected me to occurred while he was high. He always waited until my mother went to work, third shift, to turn on sexually explicit movies. Then he would call me in the room to watch with him, saying, "Let me massage you and you massage me like in the movie." We never had sex through vaginal penetration; it was always oral sex, and since I really trusted my father, I thought this was another way of showing how much I loved him and how much he loved me. Still, even as a child, something on the inside of me felt it wasn't right, but I didn't have anyone to tell,

I'm Back!

Sophia

nor did I have any other role models to show me that what was happening to me was wrong.

In the midst of those encounters, I also had to deal with my step-grandfather who loved to bounce me on his knee. He would sit me snug in his lap for long periods of time and tell me about all the women he had on the side. In other words, he talked about cheating on my grandmother. I guess I was a magnet for this abuse, and all of it seemed to start at the same time, when I was nine. I started my period and developed a chest—at age nine. I started hating myself and my body—at age

Sophia

nine. I started resenting my mother—at age nine. I lost myself—at age nine. I was raped three times between the ages of thirteen and fourteen. Each time took more of my identity and self worth. By the age of sixteen, I felt like a washed up rag. My thoughts and emotions were centered around two words: "What else?"

I'm Back!

Sophia

PSALM 27- (NIV)

The LORD is my light and my salvation - whom shall I fear? The LORD is the stronghold of my life - of whom shall I be afraid?

When evil men advance against me to devour my flesh, when my enemies and my foes attack me, they will stumble and fall.

Though an army besiege me, my heart will not fear; though war break out against me, even then will I be confident.

One thing I ask of the LORD, this is what I seek: that I may dwell in the house of the LORD all the days of my life, to gaze upon the beauty of the LORD and to seek him in his temple.

For in the day of trouble he will keep me safe in his dwelling; he will hide me in the shelter of his tabernacle and set me high upon a rock.

Then my head will be exalted above the enemies who surround me; at his tabernacle will I sacrifice with shouts of joy, I will sing and make music to the LORD

I'm Back!

Sophia

Hear my voice when I call, O LORD; be merciful to me and answer me.

My heart says of you, "Seek his face!" Your face, LORD, I will seek.

Do not hide your face from me, do not turn your servant away in anger; you have been my helper. Do not reject me or forsake me, O God my Savior.

Though my father and mother forsake me, the LORD will receive me.

Teach me your way, O LORD; lead me in a straight path because of my oppressors.

Do not turn me over to the desire of my foes, for false witnesses rise up against me, breathing out violence.

I am still confident of this: I will see the goodness of the LORD in the land of the living.

Wait for the LORD; be strong and take heart and wait for the LORD.

I'm Back!

Sophia

MYTH VS FACT

I'm Back!

MYTH 1

The primary motive for sexual assault is sexual. People who commit sexual assault do not have any other outlet for their sexual needs.

FACT

The major motive for sexual assault is **POWER**- to overpower and control another person. Rape is not about sex. It is sexualized violence, not violent sex. Three out of five offenders also are in consenting sexual relationships.

MYTH 2

The victim provokes sexual assault.

FACT

Someone's actions or dress cannot send a message "**asking**" for sexual assault. In fact, studies demonstrate that 71% of sexual assaults are planned in advance, making the survivor's demeanor or apparel at the time of the sexual assault irrelevant. It is preposterous to believe someone would ask for or enjoy a physical attack involving risks that include venereal disease, pregnancy, injury or even death.

I'm Back!

MYTH 3

Sexual assault occurs only among strangers.

FACT

Over 50% of all sexual assaults involve acquaintances or friends. A close personal friend, family member, or family friend is the offender in 14% of cases reported (a person is less likely to report sexual assault by a friend or relative).

MYTH 4

Anyone can prevent sexual assault if he/she really wants to.

FACT

This myth asserts that no one can be forced to have sex. In fact, since nearly 90% of all sexual assaults involve threats of physical harm or the actual use of physical force, it follows that a person might submit to sexual assault to prevent more severe bodily injury or death. Vulnerability to assault also increases because most women are not brought up to be physically aggressive, and they are not as strong as men.

I'm Back!

Sophia

*Information provided by *Sexual Assault Advocate Training Manual*, Texas Association Against Sexual Assault Office of the Attorney General. Revised August 2004

I'm Back!

Sophia

DECEASED INNOCENCE

I'm Back!

Sophia

How far back can you remember where life was innocent and you were care-free? I can remember when my innocence died. A piece of me died before I could even grasp the fact that it was once a part of me. I plan to have a funeral once the words of the journey are completed in this book. I'm going to have a symbolic funeral burying the hurt, abuse, loneliness, regret and guilt. I will stand on my grave, not live in it. I will stand up for the saying, "You're Worth the Wait." I used to be afraid to tell my boyfriend, "I'm not ready to have sex" because I was afraid he would leave me or not love me. What a fool! I realize now

I'm Back!

that it is an honor for someone to be with me, not the other way around. A man should feel honored to have a virtuous woman and a woman who has standards, goals, ambition and faith in God.

Sometimes, I feel I was cheated out of the "first time" experience with my 'first time' making love experience being with my husband, my best friend, my soul mate in Christ. I was cheated out of having my "first love" be the father of ALL of my children. BUT reality stands; that wasn't my first experience. My first experience was wasted on the enemy. However, I do find solace in knowing that God can give me a first time experience with my future love that will shatter the past hurts and fill the voids. My future love will be in love with God, and so I know he'll be able to stay in love with me. Wow, I'm getting excited just thinking about what's to come. Faith can do that for you, just holding on to the hope of what's to come and the things you can't quite see. Thank you, God! I give Him thanks now for what's to come. Faith is acting like it is so even though it isn't so, in order that it might be so!

I'm Back!

Sophia

Love is a whisper ©

Love is a whisper, all snug in its breath
No one can touch, because it's locked in my
chest

Love is far but I come near
To unlock the door with a faraway fear

I open my eyes with shock and surprise
To see my love has gone afar

Wait, wait I say in my mind
For I thought this was a poem
But I see that I lie

For it is my heart that yearns for love
To hold, caress and keep it above

Keep it above from all the hate for when
There is no love that's all that a waits

My love, you are the key that unlocked my heart
I'm forever grateful for being set free

I'm Back!

Sophia

Love, love, love oh how that word just becomes me.

I'm Back!

Sophia

LOST

Sophia

Given that I wasn't raised in church, I had limited spiritual awareness on which to rely. I originally came to church because a friend of mine, whom I met in the Springfield Boy's and Girls Club overnight camp, invited me to come to his church to sing in the junior choir. At eleven or twelve, I started going to church just to sing in the choir, as I fell asleep during the sermon. I didn't know what the phrase, "You're worth the wait" meant. I don't think I heard that phrase until I was in my twenties. They didn't teach that in church, where it was almost taboo to mention the word "sex."

Sophia

I remember hearing the preacher talk about fornicators, adulterers, and sinners. People seldom took the time to break it down for children and teenagers my age. The home and church should be the catalyst for our children's foundation to be set. We can't be ignorant to what our children are learning on the streets, schools and on television. Sexual innuendos are everywhere. It's our job to execute the 3 P's, as I so aggressively communicate in my speeches. PRACTICE ~PROACTIVE~ PREVENTION. When it's all said and done, I went to church faithfully and was faithfully lost.

Sophia

MYTH VS FACT

I'm Back!

Sophia

MYTH 5
It cannot happen to me or my child.

FACT
Anyone may be sexually assaulted. Studies show that victims include 6-month babies to 99-year old women and men, people of color, lesbians/gays, people with disabilities and people from every racial, ethnic, religious, economic and social background. The National Victims Center says a sexual assault occurs every 6 minutes in the US. Approximately 25%-35% of all women will be sexually assaulted. And approximately 20%-30% of all men will be victims before they are 18. Only 1 out of 10 sexual assaults are ever reported to law enforcement.

MYTH 6
Most sexual assault offenders are African American.

FACT
In 1994, Bureau of Justice, estimated that of our 33,800 imprisoned rape offenders 52.2% were white, 43.7 were black and

Sophia

4.1% were other. These figures are based on over ten years ago; however, the trend still holds true today.

MYTH 7
I would know if my child is being abused.

FACT
Most parents don't have a clue what's happening to their children because they refuse to believe that it could happen. I speak on the 3 P's of parenting. (Practice Proactive Prevention). Children aren't stupid; they're just not aware of the severity of sexual abuse. Parents should approach their children often with correct facts and not myths.

*Information provided by Sexual Assault Advocate Training Manual, Texas Association Against Sexual Assault Office of the Attorney General. Revised August 2004
*Trustworthy Consulting and Empowerment Driven by Knowledge conducts self-esteem workshops and seminars on 3P's of Parenting (Practicing Proactive Prevention) visit www.trustworthyconsult.com for more information.

I'm Back!

DEATH OF AN UNDERTAKER

Sophia

My mother, younger brother and I left my father and moved into a shelter apartment in Holyoke, MA in 1992. It was for homeless mothers and children. My father's drug habit got so out of control that we were no longer safe. Right before we moved to Holyoke, my mother kicked my father out of our apartment on Ralph Street. They were getting into knock out – drag out fights every day. I was used to seeing them fight every once in a while in West Springfield, but on Ralph Street, he was constantly high, and they were constantly fighting.

I'm Back!

Sophia

As for me, I knew I had had it the day he came to my school to pick me up. It was a fall, cold yet sunny day in 1992. He showed up at Forest Park Jr. High in his turquoise putt-putt of a car. He was drunk and playing loud music. I don't remember why he came early to get me, but he did. We lived on the second floor, and as soon as he pulled into the driveway on Ralph Street, I jumped out running, trying to get to the stairs before he did. I felt as if I were running for my life. I knew what would happen to me, but if I could lock the door, I could at least keep him away from me for a while. I was running; he was running. I didn't have time to think. I just had to make it. He grabbed my legs and pulled me down. We were going toe for toe in the stairway. He was laying on me pinning my hands down, calling me a slut. "You a ho' just like your mother," he yelled.

Still pinning me down, he told me that I would never be anything more than a ho. Screaming at the top of my lungs, I begged him to let me go. Finally, I had my chance. I kicked him in the face, and he fell down the stairs. I ran in the house and locked the down. Our electricity was off and the phone had been disconnected, so I couldn't call for help.

Sophia

When my mother finally came home with my brother, my father had come down from his drunken rage and drug induced high, but this tiny bit of peace was short lived. Before long, my parents were arguing. With their tempers raging and the screaming out of control, my baby brother and I did what we knew to do: he cried and I hid. After my mom and dad separated, things were a little better. At least there was no violence.

When the phone rang on April 22, 1993, I ran to the kitchen to grab the phone. Usually, that's what 13-year-olds lived for, the phone.

Sophia

"Hello," I said, quickly picking it up before the fourth ring.

It was Nana's voice that I heard, and I wondered what she wanted. After all, she rarely called us at the shelter apartment.

"After your father dropped Jennifer and you off, he got into a car accident, and he's dead." I dropped the phone, throwing my hands up. I looked around in fear and disbelief. I remember feeling devastated and hopeless. Not knowing what to do, I found myself running down the short, narrow hallway. I remember collapsing on the dull tile

Sophia

in the bathroom, wailing over the cold, white toilet seat.

Suddenly, it was as if I were standing outside my body, watching my life rewind. I was six years old, and my father and I were going to Riverside Park to watch the car races; Then, I was traveling with my parents in our camper. I saw us going to Cape Cod, Myrtle Beach, and New York City. Quickly, another vision prevailed. I was a little girl, fishing with my daddy. For a brief moment, I had so many happy thoughts, but then I saw it—a little girl lying down next to her father while he slept. She was only 9, and without warning, he reached over and put his hands in her pants. He started touching her, massaging her behind and other private areas, and just as suddenly as that vision came, another took its place. This little girl saw her father franticly searching for little white rocks, his crack, which dropped in the backseat while he was driving his Corvette. She could hear him calling her a slut when she was 12 years. Even though she knew it was because he was drunk and high and mad at her mother, she could still feel the twinges of pain in her heart, as if it were happening now.

I'm Back!

Sophia

Suddenly reality slapped her face. Her dad, her hero, had been clean from drugs for eight months now, and he was back in church.

"I just saw him" I cried, in disbelief. We spent the night at his apartment last night. I was supposed to go to church with him. This couldn't be. Not my dad—not my father! I loved him so much, and I can't see him ever again.

"Why me? What did I do? What are we going to do?"

I had learned to suppress so many things, even to the point of lying to make my life seem better than what it was. I can still

I'm Back!

Sophia

see my dad's bright smile, mustache over his top lip and the bald look he was going for towards the end. Despite the abuse, I always went back to all of the good memories. Perhaps it was my only defense to keep going when it seemed hopeless. He's dead and he laid the foundation for low self-esteem, deception, suicidal attempts and promiscuity. These things would follow me for the next 15 years.

Sophia

THE TRUTH HURTS

I'm Back!

Sophia

We had just buried my father at Oak Groove cemetery in Springfield, MA under a cross that just says STROTHER. And sixteen years later my grandmother still hadn't upgraded the stone to reveal the man's name that is beneath the cross. About two weeks after the funeral, my mother decided she wanted to move back to Texas to be closer to her side of the family. I was furious and hurt! How could she move me away from everything that I knew. I had just learned that my dad fathered another child, Tyrone Bailey. I was hoping that maybe my other brother Andre' Stewart, and I would finally have a chance to

I'm Back!

grow closer. We had not had time to mourn or grieve yet. I refused. I refused to move; she couldn't make me move anywhere, and I was standing my ground. I would realize later I should've left with my mother instead of thinking I knew what was best for me, a child.

I was supposed to stay with June and Glenn Forbes, a couple from church who had taken me under their wings, along with others, but I wanted to stay with my godmother, instead. That was a wrong decision, the worst one that I could have made. There was no real supervision in her home. She couldn't be in

Sophia

two places at once, and especially in this two-story home, there was abuse going on right under her nose. She was wearing so many hats that she couldn't see over the bridge of her nose. Of the girls who lived with her, several claimed to have been molested and sexually harassed. Still, none of us had the nerves to say so. We didn't feel she would give us the support we needed to come forward. In my living there less than two months, I was sexually harassed several times. After I revealed one occasion during a confrontation with her, she said, "I know it was your fault; you probably led him on."

62   I'm Back!

Sophia

I was only 13. The man was in his twenties. Who was the predator?

Two months after my father's death, I left my godmother's house for the day, just to get out of the house with my friend, Michelle. We were best friends with a capital "B." We did everything together and I truly loved her for that. She was the big sister that I never had and it was great while it lasted. We walk around the city, shoot the breeze a bit. We were not looking for trouble, just a nice time, taking it easy, enjoying the day. When we ran into the guy that she was dating, we decided to go to Springfield College and chill by the track. His brother was with him, so we found a shady tree on the King Street side of the college and sat there. Eventually, Michelle and her friend started kissing and hugging and laughing. The guy's brother started looking at me like he wanted to do the same thing. I tried to keep him occupied in conversation alone, but it's hard for a 13 year-old to keep an 18 year-old man occupied with conversation.

At that point, however, I wasn't afraid of him. I actually thought he was kind of cute. With his true chocolate skin, he had a nice smile with beautiful white teeth, and his thick accent sounded Jamaican. Thinking like a kid,

I'm Back!

Sophia

I decided to go for a short walk alone and maybe he would get a clue that I wasn't interested in making out. As I started down the grassy area, I noticed he was following me. I started to feel a bit nervous, but I never thought he would hurt me. But as I ducked behind the bushes that created a covered trail, to my surprise, he was there!

"Come on baby! You know you were feelin' me." he whispered. "No, I'm alright," I said trembling, trying to get out of his solid grip of my right hand. "I just want to go."

I tripped over a huge root that was sticking out of the ground, and with my fall, he went into full gear. Dragging me over to the far right end of the area, he pressed his body on me. We were completely isolated from public view.

"Pull your pants down."

"No, I don't want to do this." I cried softly.

Piercing his teeth into the right side of my neck, he yanked at my pants and repeated himself. "Pull down your pants! If you don't, I'll bite harder."

But I still had a little fight in me, and I refused to pull my pants down. The pain I felt after that still haunts me today. He bit my flesh

I'm Back!

off. Through his constant taunting and biting, finally, my entire body went numb. I couldn't fight anymore; there was no movement left in me. What seemed like hours was actually about two minutes. He entered my body, his face dripping in sweat. I just looked to the right and cried.

I cried and cried, as flashes of the past entered my mind. I thought of my father and grandfather. "Is this what it's all about? Am I supposed to just say 'yes' and endure this from all men?" After he ejaculated on my shirt, he helped me up, patted my clothes clean from the dirt and brush and said,

Sophia

"See that wasn't all that bad. Did you like it?" He even started fixing my hair. I started running aimlessly!

I continued to run for the next ten years. I was quick to move if things weren't going right in my life, quick to leave a relationship if I felt smothered or unhappy. I never really dealt with my issues or felt comfortable talking about them. Instead, I masked them or created a different personality so I wouldn't have to deal with them. Even today, I feel uncomfortable when someone tries to hug or kiss the right side of my neck. I have to deliberately deal with my fear and have faith that God will work

I'm Back!

them out for me spiritually, mentally and emotionally.

I've never really gone into the details with my god mother, but I've learned not to blame her entirely for some of the dealings that went on in and out of her home. I've learned that there's not a parent manual that is absolute and binding for all parenting situations however we do need to pay more attention to our children and their surroundings. Children talk even without saying a word sometimes. They may start a new habit or change an existing habit based upon things going on in their life. Pay

Sophia

attention to the small details in their lives and ask questions. You have not because you ask not!

I'm Back!

Sophia

IS IT A NEW DAY?

Sophia

Years later, I find myself staring into

the sunlight through my window daydreaming

about a life without drama and pain. I slowly

rise from my bed walking to the window, ever

so cautiously and calmly. My left hand

precedes me, reaching for the sunlight

embracing the energy that is beaming through

the glass. As I touch the glass, I'm

immediately stopped in my grasp because I

can't go any further. Something is in my way—

blocking my reach for the sunlight.

Something! It is my past. My past is that

glass on the window. My past is that barrier

from my future.

I'm Back!

Sophia

Here I go again with the question, "Why?" Why do I find myself crying about another relationship gone wrong? How do I manage to find myself in dysfunctional relationships? What is wrong with me where I allow myself to entertain men that I know scream RED FLAG? Who is going to save me from myself? When will I get a clue?

One relationship after another I find myself empty and drained. Either I am trying to change someone or create the ONE. I find myself giving of myself too quickly and too easily. WHY? I leave relationships praying they won't tell anyone about us. WHY?

I'm Back! 73

Sophia

What's wrong with Sophia? Is it the fact that I'm a single parent? Is it the fact that I don't like to communicate my true feelings?

Sex is just sex to me. It's not some special connection between two people who love each other and call it "Making Love." It was just something I thought was a part of any relationship, especially if the man did nice things for me—almost like the old fashioned barter system. Since I was introduced to sex by my father at an early age, I just assumed it was another way to show my appreciation or my obligation to a man. I really didn't realize it was my CHOICE. As I reflect, I realize I made

I'm Back!

some really stupid decisions as an adolescent because I didn't know about CHOICES. Someone said to me "Sophia you just made some bad decisions" and I replied "How could I have made bad decisions, if I never knew what a good one was?" Losing my virginity wasn't about waiting on marriage or the ONE. It was about peer pressure and not wanting to be the odd one.

It's funny that I was considered not cool because I hadn't had sex with a guy on my own accord. I remember clearly as if it was yesterday. I was living on Ralph Street in Springfield, MA. My mother, as always, didn't

Sophia

really care what I did, and I was able to stay out in the neighborhood late. I was hanging out with two of my friends from the church that I went to. They were going to spend the night with me. We were out playing hiding go get… not seek… with some of the neighborhood kids.

While we were going to hide one of the girls kept egging me on: "I can't believe you haven't had sex yet; girl you better do it and join the club. It's great!" I kept laughing and trying to play it off by saying "It's not all of that." I'd been introduced when I was nine and here I am 13 being reintroduced to sex as if it was some initiation ceremony. Both friends had been sexually active for some time and were a few years older than I was. I didn't want to be known as the girl who wasn't cool enough for the group or was scared to have sex. How crazy and powerful peer pressure and influence can be when you don't have any family values or a support system at home.

So I had made up in my mind tonight was going to be the night of vindication and acceptance. With my knees shaking, stomach turning and mind racing, I allowed myself to be found by a boy that was hot for me. We went to the back of my house next to the garage and started making out. After the first 10 minutes of kissing and hugging, I said, "Let's stop. I don't really feel right, not out here, not like this."

He kept saying in my ear, "No let's just go ahead; I know you want to." It was so passionate but so wrong; however, I kept hearing my friend's voice in my ear saying, "Just do it. Come on, join us. You'll be one of us."

I still couldn't comfortably go through with it. I just felt dirty doing this outside with someone whom I really didn't like. But he was so relentless; he kept fondling me and trying to

I'm Back!

unzip my pants. After about 25 minutes of just third base…it happened. While he was trying to penetrate, I cried because it hurt so badly. I told him please stop. "This isn't right!"

He finally got how serious I was and stopped. I hid for most of the night, but who was I hiding from? I wasn't ashamed that my Mom might find out. I was ashamed that it was done outside on the ground. I felt like a dirty dog. I felt worthless and cheap.

I just kept rocking and whispering, "I can't take this back; it's done. Will I be one of them, the girls, even though I didn't finish?"

Sophia

Once I came out of my fog of disbelief I went to find the others, looking for some embracing and once I saw them I couldn't bring myself to admit my failing. I had failed to completely follow through. But from that moment on having sex wasn't some sacred and cherished act it was just something to do to feel accepted. Everything that led up to it was what I did with my father to feel accepted by him so it would be what I needed to do to be accepted by my boyfriend...right?

Where was my mother in all of this? Why didn't she have me in the house as soon

I'm Back!

as the lights went out? Why didn't she come out looking for me once 11:00pm hit? Why didn't she ask me where have you been? Why hadn't she had that talk about birds and the bees? Why hadn't she sat me down to teach me how to love myself and cherish my temple? Why hadn't she noticed that dad and I were spending too much time together? WHY? I have so many questions for my mother. I truly feel she has failed me in so many ways. For so many years I hated my mother for not protecting me from my dad, grandfather, boys and myself. Then she get's hooked on crack and try's to sell me or leverage me for her drugs. What kind of mother allows her daughter to endure such hell and then expects her to love her unconditionally. It's amazing that for years I never knew my mother was on drugs and lived with her. Especially after my father died in 1993 that's when my mother's drug habit got out of control. Two weeks after his death my mother packed up my baby brother and moved to Marlin Texas. I refused to go I wanted to stay close to my father's grave and my friends. But she left anyway and I joined her July 1993 after getting raped at Springfield College and sexually harassed by others at

I'm Back!

Sophia

my godmother's house. I remember my move to Marlin summer of 1993; I was 13 years old freshman in high school. Boy was I gullible, naive and a target for predators. My mother was distant and still grieving deeply. We moved in with my deceased grandfather in Marlin while she looked for a place to live. My grandfather was something else; he was a short man in statue but had a very large personality and had a contagious smile. He also had a very good memory. On this one occasion when I was nine years old, my mother sent me to Marlin to visit my grandmother and grandfather. While I was there, my grandfather told me NOT to touch the Blue Bell ice cream that was in the deep freezer. BUT being 9 and ooh so tempted by the vanilla Blue Bell ice cream, I snuck a scoop while he was taking a nap. To my shock and surprise once he got up he checked the ice cream and to his dismay and frustration he found a big scoop GONE. You would've thought I stole his wallet or cigar; he was hot! I could hear him calling me outside. I ran to my grandmother, who was my protector. Of course, I had to start crying so I could get my grandmother on my side. Then out came my

I'm Back!

grandfather standing all but 5'3 or 5'4, slender with a fresh low cut Afro yelling, "I told you not to touch my ice cream! Get over here now!"

I was pleading for my life…when I knew it wasn't that serious but I didn't want the spanking that I knew I deserved. But after a few minutes of calming, my grandmother convinced him to not spank me but to just put me in time out without TV for a while. To make a long story short, up until his death in 2003 he NEVER let me forget the time I stole his Blue Bell ice cream. Mind you I was 23 when he passed.

Sophia

As I mentioned earlier when we first moved to Texas we lived with my grandfather for four months and then moved to Waco. In those four months, I was the target of continuous advances by the men in Marlin, young and old. I was new, fresh and untouched. Every day I endured constant sexually advances from every direction. I didn't know how to handle all of the pressure and attention. I always knew I was thicker than the average girl my age but I didn't realize that I had features that were more womanly than "girly." I was quiet and somewhat of a loner. I tended to hang with

I'm Back!

the same group of people and barely spent time with my mother. Once I came home she was gone until it was time for me to go to school in the morning.

When we moved to Waco, I didn't get as much attention, which was nice and comforting. I was able to focus on school more, and I really liked Waco 9th Grade Center a lot. Unfortunately, that was short lived because my mother moved back to Marlin in the summer of 1994 to live in one of my grandfather's houses. The next 15 months of my life was truly a living hell, and they forever changed me. My mom was about 5 or 6

Sophia

months pregnant and wasn't really sure who the father was. Prior to getting pregnant, she was dating about 3 or 4 different guys and had to narrow the list down based on which week she was with the guy to figure who she was pregnant by. I lost so much respect for my mother during that period because most of the men she brought around always tried to have sex with me including the man that ended up being the father of my younger brother. Gross I know, but unfortunately, this has been my reality for a lifetime.

Sophia

Once back in Marlin, I called myself dating one of the football players who was very popular. He was actually a gentleman and wasn't trying to get in my pants all the time. Remember I was still only 14 years old. I was a sophomore in high school dating a senior who was 18 years. He mesmerized me, and I was proud that I was his girl. I didn't care that I heard he was messing around with someone else; I just loved the attention he gave me. We actually waited a couple of months before we became intimate, which was considered a long time in that setting. You must realize in Marlin, there were only a few things for young people to do after

school…have sex, drink, smoke, go to a club

or party and the game room.   Toward the end

of my mother's pregnancy, I didn't get out

much. I was home helping her a lot; however,

two weeks after she had my other younger

brother, I got out!

    I was with a girl from town, and we were

just walking. There was nothing to do as

always, and while we were out, we saw her

boyfriend and his friend. We shot the breeze

outside for a while and then decided to go to

his house. We sat outside a little more and

talked, laughed and anticipated the next move.

I'm Back!

Sophia

Her boyfriend invited us in, and they went in
the other room, I suspect to make out. That
left his friend and me to look at each other,
wondering what we were going to do. I had
known his friend from school in the past; he
was very well known in the town and known
for his ability to play ball; however, he'd gotten
mixed up in the drug life. I could feel his
desire for me mounting through his relentless
glaring. He'd made passes at me in the past,
but I would just laugh and keep walking
wherever I was going. But this time I couldn't
just laugh and walk anywhere. I'd come with
my friend, and she was in the other room

probably making out with her boyfriend. So

what could I do to get out of this one? At any

rate, he didn't waste much time. His glare

turned into immediate action. First he moved

in for the kill by sliding closer and smelling my

neck and then whispering into my ear. The

whisper quickly turned into a touch and the

touch a kiss. I allowed the kiss so he took that

as the official go ahead, but I knew I didn't

want to go all the way. Still, as always, here I

was in a predicament where a guy is

relentless, and I'm getting weary holding him

off. We struggled, but for some ridiculous

I'm Back!

reason, he thought it was part of the foreplay or shall I say rough play.

I kept saying, "I don't want to do this. Please, this doesn't feel right," but he kept moving forward closer, and closer and then eventually he penetrated me, literally for one minute. Then I said to myself, "Enough is enough." I pushed him back and said with aggression, "No! This doesn't feel right." And it was done. I finally mustered a little bit of strength to show aggression with my "No." I stood up for myself. I didn't want to have sex and I don't want to wake up AGAIN regretting not standing up for myself.

Sophia

Four weeks later though I noticed something was wrong. I was getting my period. What's going on? I can't be pregnant. My boyfriend and I had sex but it was with a condom.   I know it's not by the guy that I made get off me…it was too quick, right? WRONG, I was PREGNANT! "Oh my gosh! What am I'm going to do?" I was fourteen years old, and pregnant by someone I wasn't even with and didn't even want to have sex with. I was already taking care of my two younger brothers— full time because my mother was out all times of night everyday. We didn't have money or room.

I'm Back!

Sophia

"What am I going to do?"

I decided to get rid of it. That was my quick remedy for a very unwanted pregnancy. I tried everything in my power from starting fights, belly flopping on the ground, running into doorknobs, drinking, smoking weed and the ultimate, to get an abortion! I told my boyfriend at the time, the senior, I was pregnant by him because I honestly thought he was the father. Maybe the condom broke or he didn't put it on right. I couldn't be pregnant by this other guy, right? It was too quick and unwanted. It couldn't be the other guy who I pushed off me, and it only lasted literally 60 seconds. It just couldn't…or could

it? I was able to hide the pregnancy for 6

months from my mother and then the bump

started to show. She didn't have any words or

feelings. I don't remember any

debate…nothing. She said we'll get money

from Nana and his parents to help pay for a

late term abortion and you'll be all set. So

that's what we did; we got $1200 combined

and headed to Dallas for the procedure. The

only thing we weren't counting on was God

being in the midst.

So here we were in Dallas and I was on

the examining table. I was 15 years old and 6

months pregnant, getting a pre-op exam and the nurse said, "I'm sorry dear, but we can't proceed. You're 2 weeks too far for the procedure." I began to wail, thinking to myself, "My life is completely over." We headed back to Marlin feeling defeated and desolate. I went to my doctor in Marlin for another check up and when they did the exam, he said, "They miscalculated your term. You could've had the late term abortion."

At that point, I knew that God had another plan for the life that was growing within me. From then on I just accepted my fate and this life that was coming. From then

on I knew this child was destined by God.
Once Zavier was born on July 9, 1995, my life
changed forever. I, for once, had a true
purpose and passion to escape the grips of my
mother. I, for once, had a true love I could call
my own. I, for once, had a reason to live. I,
for once, had a chance to show a man real
love and how to love a woman unconditionally
for her and not her body. Zavier gave me the
strength to question my mother and her
activities. He gave me the strength to want a
better in life and to finish my education. I
never wanted to give him a reason not to
succeed or be hurt as a result of my actions.

I'm Back!

Sophia

He gave me a reason to be everything my

mother wasn't. He gave me life.

I'm Back!

Sophia

IS THE DOCTOR IN?

I'm Back!

Sophia
Mark 5:25-34(NIV)

A large crowd followed and pressed around him. And a woman was there who had been subject to bleeding for twelve years. She had suffered a great deal under the care of many doctors and had spent all she had, yet instead of getting better she grew worse. When she heard about Jesus, she came up behind him in the crowd and touched his cloak, because she thought, "If I just touch his clothes, I will be healed." Immediately her bleeding stopped and she felt in her body that she was freed from her suffering.

At once Jesus realized that power had gone out from him. He turned around in the crowd and asked, "Who touched my clothes?"

"You see the people crowding against you," his disciples answered, "and yet you can ask, 'Who touched me?' "

I'm Back!

Sophia

But Jesus kept looking around to see who had done it. Then the woman, knowing what had happened to her, came and fell at his feet and, trembling with fear, told him the whole truth. He said to her, "Daughter, your faith has healed you. Go in peace and be freed from your suffering."

This story in the Bible just reigns true for my personal testimony. I've been plagued with low self-esteem, loneliness, guilt and depression for years. And I realized if I could just touch the hem of His garment, I could be made whole. I cry out to Jesus please allow me to love myself more than anyone else. I cry out to Jesus please allow me to love you more than myself. Lord, I cry out please allow me to get out of my grave and LIVE. I'm sick of wallowing six feet under, it's time to ascend seven (completion or it's over)feet and then eight (New beginnings, your free) feet. The sky isn't the limit!

Your plague can be any thing that has influence over you or is hindering you. Most of the time we go to the wrong physicians for our problems. We seek sex as a means for healing if we're lacking love from our parents or peers. We seek gangs and clicks if we feel like outcasts. We seek drugs or alcohol if we feel void or need to experiment a new high. We never seek Jesus until we've exhausted all the wrong physicians. If we seek Jesus first,

I'm Back! 103

cry out to Him first, lean on Him first we won't have to waste years and money finding the right fix or getting second and third doctor's opinions from the enemy. The enemy desires to sift us as wheat and use any method possible to delay or destroy what God has for us and has for us to do. Press your way through to the ultimate Physician and leave these unlicensed doctors alone. All you have to do is say the following out loud and believe in your heart:

Lord, I thank you for my life, health and strength. I believe that you are the Lord Jesus Christ. I believe that You rose from

I'm Back!

the dead to reign in Heaven. Lord, forgive me of all of my sins and help me to learn how to live Holy. I believe that you died to save me. In Jesus Name, Amen.

Romans 10:9, 10 states "That if thou shalt confess with thy mouth the Lord Jesus, and shalt believe in thine heart that God hath raised him from the dead, thou shalt be saved. For with the heart man believeth unto righteousness; and with the mouth confession is made unto salvation.

I'm Back!   105

MOTHER, MOTHER

WHERE ART THOU?

I'm Back!

Sophia

The last wordless page indicates the absence of my mother for the first 10 years of my life. I don't remember much about my mother outside of the fact that she worked nights and slept during the days as she worked as a caregiver for elderly that had some sort of mental retardation. When I look back I sometimes resent my mother for not protecting me from my father and other predators. I say "How could she not have known or did she and did nothing?" I didn't really have a relationship with my mother until the age of 10 when my father succumbed to drugs. I can remember my mother, baby

Sophia

brother and I walking the streets of West Springfield and Holyoke looking for open pantries and goodwill type shops trying to get a hot meal and free clothes. I remember living on Ralph Street with no electricity and facing homelessness. I remember living in a shelter while in the 8th grade and going to school everyday pretending as if I had the best life ever. But I also remember doing the majority of our household chores before dusk and then using candles and flashlights in the evening. I remember most nights how we went to bed early so we didn't have to deal with the darkness and hunger. I can remember when

I'm Back!

Sophia

we moved to Texas after my fathers' death,
my mother would have me call my Nana and
lie about not having electricity or food so she
could get my Nana to send money and then
she would use it to support her drug habit.

My mother and I have had a turbulent
relationship. A true love - hate thing. The
saying is thin line between love and hate and
that proves true in any relationship. I love my
mother just because she gave birth to me
however I hate the demon that she became.

My life has been plagued with those that
were supposed to protect me however they
were absent or astray. My mother flirted with

drugs and sex for a long time and ultimately passing the consequences onto me. Proverbs 22:6 can't reign true if you continually "...bring your children to wrath." It's sad to know that your mother hates you because you defied the odds and lived. She's jealous of everything that she's not. Yes, I feel my mother owes me an apology sometimes. Think about it, she smoked weed in front of me and with me. She smoked crack with my son's father while stealing from me to support her habit. She has allowed MEN to sexually, mentally and physically abuse me while she selfishly indulged in her own desires.

I'm Back!

Sophia

Wait! I know that I need to recognize spiritually that this wasn't my mother; Instead, it was the demons inside of her. I found that to be easier said then done, however. How do I separate the two, flesh and spirit, good and evil, demon and angel when I see mom? Deceased innocence is not about one man killing a child's soul; deceased innocence is about Jesus being able to resurrect what Satan couldn't kill through my parents. I feel sorry for my mother because outside of my two younger brothers who I helped to raise while she ran the streets, she's alone—fifty

I'm Back!

and nothing to show for it except three children.

Someone used to tell me to remember that there's always someone going through something three times worst than my situation. That saying is so true. I say to God sometimes, "Lord, when can I catch a break?"

I'm trying to live accordingly, love my enemies, keep Him first and it seems as though it's still not getting me anywhere. I'm still two checks behind my bills. I'm still a couple of dollars from being homeless. What will I do if I lost my job? Even when I put the pen to the paper, I'm thinking those same

I'm Back!

thoughts. I want to be debt free financially and I would like to pass on an inheritance to my children. I desire to do world-wide ministry to encourage people to look beyond their circumstance and to love themselves as Jesus loves them. I desire to have continuous peace of mind and joy and laughter in my life. The Bibles tells us if our ways are pleasing to God, He will grant us the desires of our hearts. When we pray, God generally gives three answers YES, NO or WAIT. What would God say about your ways? I forgive my mother and love her from a distance because I don't want my grave to keep me bound.

I'm Back!

Sophia

It's amazing how God will allow us to help those who despitefully used us. Just when I thought this chapter of my life wouldn't change, in February of 2008, I received a call from my mother. She was in tears as she claimed she desired a change for her life and for my two younger brothers, Aunri - and Francois. I told her to leave everything, trust God and come back to Texas.

"I will help you get back on your feet," I said and with God's providence and mercy, He allowed me the patience and love to help my mother move back to Texas. I helped her start her own catering business, Sophia's Euro

Sophia

Cuisine, a life long dream. My children now have the relationship with her, and I believe that God has truly allowed me to survive so I can help my mother live. As much as I wanted to hang on to the past hurts, lies and disappointments, when I look at my mother clean, smiling and healthy, I just thank God for His mercy and grace. Everybody deserves another chance to make things right and to live life without people hanging their past mistakes over them. I finally got the apology that I yearned to hear for so many years. I finally got the vindication that everything that I had been through was not my fault. I finally got to

Sophia

let go of the past and live for the future, never forgetting what I went through but living through what I thought I could never get over.

Sophia

THAT NAME...GOD

Sophia

One day while completing my Masters degree at American International College in 2003 I started to wonder "Why" again. Not to complain but to really reflect on how GOOD GOD is! How much I had really been through during my young years and how God never let me die in my ignorance. God has endowed me with the gift of poetry and whenever I'm going through something major in my life I start writing. I wrote this poem to sum up my true reflection and feelings about That Name… God.

This piece of poetry and heart can be applied to anyone who ever wonders "WHY."

I'm Back!

Sophia

When it comes down to it, "WHY" doesn't even matter because I'm glad that "The righteous cry and the Lord heareth, and delivereth them out of all their troubles. The Lord is nigh unto them that are of broken heart; and saveth such as be of a contrite spirit. Many are the afflictions of the righteous: but the Lord delivereth him out of them all." Psalm 34:17-19

I'm Back!

Sophia

That Name... God ©

God... What does that name really mean to me? God is who, what, why and how I breathe. My whole existence is manifested from His very name. The artistic nature of my physical being is because of His image. My chance for salvation and eternal life is because the Word was with God and the Word was God. The Word was given guidance by God to come down to suffer and save a retch like me.

Why me? Why did God choose me? Why did God see fit to create me to look like this? What inspired His creative mind to give me skin of bronze and shoulder length hair with an abundance of body to

I'm Back!

match the fullness of my lips and cheeks? Why did He decide to make me so beautiful?

How did He decide that I would be born to Sophia Jones and Andre' Strother? What made Him decide that even though my parents did not seek His face that He would keep me alive to seek His face? Why send the latter rain of protection and shelter when my parents were fighting a demon that they couldn't defeat? Why expose me to strength and will to defeat the same demon?

God has been so good to me. Despite my evil ways. Despite my horrible decisions to please the flesh. Despite all the fornication. Despite the lies. Despite the hatred in my heart. Despite turning my back on Him. Despite **MYSELF**.

His grace and mercy never grow weary. He has a genuine concern for my health and spiritual prosperity. He has an intellect that shatters all known fact or science those mere men could ever imagine. He is the I AM—everywhere all the time.

Love...a word that comes and goes but few people really know what it means to really love somebody but God reveals His love to me and gives me everything more than I could ever dream.

I'm Back!

Sophia

My life is because of God, so God means everything to ME!

Sophia

ROAD OF LIFE

I'm Back!

Sophia

Road of Life ©

The road is windy and the path sometimes rough. There maybe a detour or it may just caution us. We encountered some pot holes and bypassed some bumps. All in all we've all just begun. Our instructions were made plain but our sins made them complicated. Our map was laid out but somehow we still can't construe them. Construe which direction should reign true. We make pit stops that weren't scheduled. We thrive on unleaded when we've been afforded the Super. Super, super, supernatural power, higher, higher…the higher we travel up the road the harder it gets to stay on the strait and narrow.

The more we notice the scenery on both sides of the path; the more enticing that thought of the world than the road to Jesus becomes. Oh, yes this is the road to Jesus. There's always a piece of us that wants to hear Him say "Well Done" but so few of us that want to endure the ride to hear Him say it. The slang is perfect 'Ride or Die'. Ride with the spirit of God or die in the flesh of man. Life is defined by the

I'm Back!

Sophia

ride. The ride is defined by us. We are defined by the map. Does yours reign true?

Sophia

DAD, IS THAT YOU?

I'm Back!

Sophia

I would have never imagined myself a mother of three, divorced and starting over again all at the tender age of 27. But you never imagine yourself not living out some fairy tale existence either, especially when you are young. I started writing this memoir just a year into my marriage and by year two, I had filed for divorce and had to fight for everything I'd worked hard to achieve, including a child that almost cost me my life.

The relationship beginnings of my ex-husband and I are a bit complicated. We met in 1998 while he was married but separated from his wife. I was 18 and he was 38. He

Sophia

pursued me by filling all of the voids I had experienced growing up. We broke it off about 3 months later because his wife miraculously wanted to salvage their marriage once she caught wind of our relationship.

My ex-husband had known my family for years and as I found out later, he knew them *intimately.* In the fall of 2003, he called me up out of the blue claiming that I was on his mind and he wanted to see how I was doing. That phone call turned into a seven month courtship with marriage following in September of 2004. I'm mature enough to admit I married for the wrong reasons. Even though I thought at the

I'm Back!

time the marriage might last, deep inside I was fearful to voice that I had second thoughts from the very beginning. My ex-husband was 20 years my senior and had a previous intimate encounter within my family. I had no knowledge of this relationship until two weeks before my wedding, after I was already pregnant. I felt there was no way out with his aggressive courtship and my grandmother's strong influence of old school teaching. Yes, my grandmother played a major part in my decision to get married. One day I drove up to her house and I asked what she thought of my calling off the wedding, she replied, "Sophia, don't be stupid. You mess up everything; don't mess this up. He will take care of you and bring stability to you and the children. Don't be stupid!"

Her comment, in addition to one other factor that drew me to my soon-to-be husband, pretty much sealed the decision to go on with the wedding. What was that other factor? He resembled my father tremendously—same complexion, same grade of hair, same nose and same personality. I now realize that I was overwhelmed with the fatherly aspect his age brought to the relationship, and with the charm and chivalry that he brought to the relationship as well. I thought stability would accompany his age and maybe some unforeseen wisdom; however, I soon realized that the things I ignored in the beginning would come back to haunt me.

I realize, too, that I had some personal issues within myself that I had never addressed. Of course, they started to resurface during our marriage as times we getting tough. Still, I continued to run from the truth and wallow in the lies, and I put on the mask of what happiness should be.

But God will turn the bad and make it function for our good. The journey out of my grave started with my divorce. It was a nasty and lengthy departure, but it was the rebirth of my life. Today, I look into my heart, and I thank my ex-husband, the father of my child, for allowing me to see my worth, for influencing my self-esteem because I realized it's not about remaining miserable to please someone else. I know that I am worth the wait, and I can truly love myself without allowing a man to dictate my identity. I was able to realize the faults that I held in the relationship. I realize I didn't communicate my apprehensions in the beginning. I realize I didn't communicate my disappointments

Sophia

during the relationship. I realize I failed to have a realistic look at how relationships take hard work and commitment on both ends. I realize now that pre-marital counseling is key, especially for young couples or previously divorced couples. This helps to open your minds to the reality of marriage and it helps to give different and healthy means for communication. Planning your marriage is more important than planning a dream wedding. A wedding is for a moment and you want to last a lifetime. Also I realized that if you've been abused YOU MUST DEAL WITH YOUR PAST before embracing your future

Sophia

with a mate. Trust me, you may think that if you don't talk about the past abuse or hurts that they've somehow disappeared but that's a MYTH. I had to get a divorce to realize how much of my past was lingering in my present. I didn't communicate for the fear of his reaction which was a direct link to the fear inserted into me by my father. I kept my feelings dormant and unfortunately that allowed for them to fester until 'BOOM' they exploded in a fury of bitterness, hatred and resentment. This is deadly whenever you are trying to work through a relationship or reconcile because you can't see beyond this wall of dormant feelings. I've learned I don't need to have the last word. This can be crucial in eliminating unnecessary arguments and sleepless nights. Sometimes it's best to just AGREE TO DISAGREE as they say. If you have stated your point or made your comment and your mate still doesn't understand or agree just say "Ok hun, how was work again". I know funny huh? But again you realize when you've hit a block just move on and focus on something else. Remember, don't sweat the small things. A lot of issues evolve from small disagreements that escalate into major arguments that linger for days, weeks or even months. Also, don't go to bed angry. My reasoning is I may want some 'love' time but on a more serious note it's not healthy and it's unnecessary. Take the time to hear each other out and agree that ok let's squash this or resolve this so we can go to bed TOGETHER and willing to wake up with an open mind and ready to tackle the new day adventures to come. Lastly, ladies this one is for you...Let the men be the MAN in the relationship. Most women miss out on their true blessing because they are too busy being independent and spending less time allowing

I'm Back!

their man be the HEAD (If he has a clear purpose and vision for your family and you). Listen, before you twist your lips to the side…Every HEAD needs a NECK to be supported and held upright. It also needs the NECK to turn left, right, up or down. Get this ladies, we were created from man to be a help or should I say support. We are the NECK that supports the HEAD and can ultimately help the HEAD to turn in a direction we help to foster. For example, have you ever had a situation where you may have made a recommendation to your man to do something and at the time they didn't see it your way or didn't acknowledge your suggestion. However, a few days later they woke up with a bright new idea that mirrored your previous day suggestion. Well most women would say "Well I said that to you a couple of days ago" however the correct response should be "Wow, honey that was a great idea, I'm here to support you". It really doesn't matter if you get credit. What matters is that you helped to facilitate an idea that will ultimately benefit the family or you. Ladies, remember if you take care of him, he will always take care you and your desires.

I'm Back!

Sophia

MY JOURNEY FROM THE

GRAVE

~ PEOPLE PLANTING

UNKNOWINGLY~

I'm Back!

Sophia

My father dug the hole for my casket.

My mother helped to keep me bound by the hole. God had to bring me back home to Springfield, Massachusetts in October 2007 for me to receive what He has been trying to tell me for the past few years while I was in Texas. Once again, it's amazing how we'll run from the truth and wallow in the lies.

Everyday we plant seeds. There have been many who have planted seeds in my life, and I've watered them. As a result, God allowed the increase. Remember that you reap what you sow whether it is good or bad. God gave us the command to be fruitful and

I'm Back!

Sophia

multiply the earth. We need to be fruitful in all that we do for God; Love, joy, peace, longsuffering, gentleness, goodness, faith, meekness, and temperance are all characteristics of the fruit of the Spirit. "As we have therefore opportunity, let us do good unto all men, especially unto them who are of the household of faith." (Galatians 6:10)

Thank you Aunt Sonia, Prophetess Ondrea Griffin, Prophet Kevin Williams, Bishop Craig Baymon, Pastor Essie Wilder, April Milner, Pastors Hubert and Jacquelyn Powell, Stephanie Babio, Keona Smith, and last, but not least, Nana "Mattie" Jones (Vivienne E. Strother Adams). All of you allowed God to use you as vessels for my deliverance, especially on the week of October 1, 2007.

Sonia Jones, my mother's baby sister, watched over my children while I flew to Massachusetts. She encouraged me to go and get away. You've always been there for me and the kids without murmuring or complaining. Hopefully, I've made you proud.

Ondrea Griffin stopped me in mid conversation, while visiting her and her husband in New York, to allow God to minister

Sophia

to me through her giving me confirmation and direction. Thank you for planting a seed of urgency and expectation.

Prophet Kevin Williams preached a word from on high at the Latter Rain Conference that gave me the strength to break the generational curse and focus my attention to the true source of my life…God.

Bishop Craig Baymon preached on Wednesday night of the Latter Rain Conference and confirmed my personal testimony scripture, Philippians 4:13: "I can do all things thru Christ which strengthenth me."

Sophia

Pastor Essie Wilder never withholds what God wants her to say. She confirmed the completion of this book so I can bury my past peacefully—reminding me that it's not about what I went through; it's about God allowing it so I can bring someone else through.

April Milner, my true to the heart friend, sister and confidant, never judged my faults or mistakes but prayed for me to realize what God has for my ministry. I love her for being a friend that I can count on to tell me the truth even if it hurts the flesh while setting free the spirit.

I'm Back!

Sophia

Pastor Hubert and Jacquelyn Powell hosted the Latter Rain Conference. They listened to God and brought in the men of God that eventually helped to set me free spiritually. I am also grateful to them for being true examples that I could mirror as a tool that helped me grow spiritually.

Stephanie Babio Jones affectionately known as Creola. I love you dearly and will forever regard you as my true sister.

Keona Smith is my ATL sister. We've both been through a lot and even though it's been about nine years since we've seen each other, whenever we talk, I feel like you're sitting right across from me laughing, crying and praying with me.

Last but not least, I thank God for Nana (Vivienne E. Strother Adams), affectionately known as "Mattie Jones." Thank you for being willing to set your golden years aside to undergird what God is doing in my life—to see like Mary, mother of Jesus, did that God has a greater plan than your own. You've sacrificed so much to make sure that my children and I are safe and secure mentally, emotionally, financially and spiritually. I thank you for stepping up when my father died and my

Sophia

mother couldn't break free from the demons that haunted her for so long.

Sophia

TODAY...I LEAVE THE

CEMETERY

TODAY I LIVE!

I'm Back!

Sophia

It started with my journey to the cemetery at a very young age. Before I realized it, my grave was dug. I lived six feet under for fifteen years when I finally realized there wasn't much room for me to live alongside guilt, loneliness, past hurts, sex, lies and deceit. I began to cry out for Jesus as I felt Him in my dreams. He helped me to climb out from below the grave. I then started shoveling the dirt over the hurt, loneliness, lies and deception. Immediately, the burdens began to lift. I danced on the plot and stood over the grave. God quietly called me away and said, "Your faith has made you whole. Go and be free."

I don't have to continue to dig up my past. I don't have to continue to be ashamed of my past. It's the past and I'm looking forward to my future.

I am now free to think about my future love. He will be in love with God, and so I know he'll be able to stay in love with me. Wow, I'm getting excited just thinking about what's to come. Faith can do that for you, just holding on to the hope of what's to come and the things you can't quite see. Faith is acting like it is so even though it isn't so, in order that

Sophia

it might be so!   Thank you, God!   I give Him

thanks now for what's to come!

Sophia

REALITY CHECK

I'm Back!

Sophia

We as victims need to seek counseling for the tragedies committed against us. If not we will subconsciously take our hurt out on those closest to us, especially men. For example, I know a woman who was raped and molested as a child. She never sought counseling and went on through life never admitting that she had any barriers as a result. She had two girls and later married a wonderful man. However, as time passed she started to have flashbacks of her past. Certain things her husband said or did reminded her of the predator from her youth. After a while she started to despise her husband for those memories and treated him as the predator.

Instead of talking about her feelings and concerns she shut down. She didn't want to touch him or talk to him. He was now the enemy. After a few years of simply being 'roommates,' they separated and divorced. After her divorce she realized how she should've communicated her true feelings with him, as well as her past so he could understand her actions and purposely make an effort to avoid certain trigger points.

Being abused in any way can permanently leave a mark if we don't address

I'm Back!

it. We are not superhuman where we can just shove these issues in a box and leave them for life. Eventually, the box will unravel and our issues will be exposed. I had a major issue with communication and compromise. Instead of communicating my true feelings, especially if I thought it might hurt the other person, I would keep them bottled up. I've entered into numerous relationships I really didn't want to be in simply because I was too scared to say anything or too foolish to bailout when I saw the "RED FLAGS." People have asked me if I regret some of my decisions. I used to answer, "I can't regret what I didn't think was wrong." However at what point do you start taking responsibilities for your actions and decisions.

I thought having sex was an expected and normal part of a relationship. I was introduced to sex at the age of 9. Remember— sex to me was just another thing, not a sacred experience. That element was stolen from me at a very young age. I didn't learn for a long time that our temple, body, vessels are sacred and worth real love. I'm almost thirty, and I'm still learning not to compromise for temporary pleasure or for a

Sophia

flawed perception of love. If a man truly loves a woman, he's proud of her in daylight and through the front door. I recently had to let someone know that "I'm not a back door chick – where I'm good enough to come through your back door but not your front!"

It also means I'm good enough to come through your back door where no one can see me, but I'm not good enough to leave through the front where everyone knows we're together. These are things I've struggled with for years …allowing men to have their cake and eat it too. All the while I was suffering silently. I had to realize that I am a good woman despite my past. I'm worth daylight love not just evening, in the dark love. I had to believe that my true love is looking for me right now getting ready to find me any day now.

Don't allow sex to be a common denominator in your life and relationships. Let it be sacred once again. Everyone doesn't deserve you, only the ONE that God has chosen for you. Do I have regrets? No. I am who I am today because of the good, bad and oh so ugly decisions. Now that I realize I still had issues stemming from my abuse, it's my duty to seek help so I can address those places

I'm Back!

Sophia

that need true and divine healing. Becoming a survivor is an everyday process. It takes everyday to fall in love with yourself again. It takes everyday to learn how to walk away. It takes everyday to grow your faith. It takes everyday to heal that broken place. It takes everyday to learn how to pray. It takes everyday to want to say YES. And everyday God can make it OKAY.

Sophia

STATISTICS

I'm Back!

Sophia

REAL STATISTICS...

- Around the world at least 1 women in 3 has been beaten, coerced into sex or otherwise abused in her lifetime. Most often the abuser is a member of her own family. *(John Hopkins School of Public Health 2000)*
- An estimated 91% of victims of rape are female, 9% are male and 99% of offenders are male. *(Bureau of Justice Statistics 1999)*
- 77% of rapes are committed by someone known to the person raped. *(Bureau of Justice Statistics 1997)*
- According to the National Crime Victimization Survey there were an estimated 248,000 rapes and sexual assaults against victims over the age of 12 in the US in 2001. *(US Department of Justice)*
- According to the National Victim Center, 683,000 women are raped each year. *(1992)*
- Only 2% of rapists are convicted and imprisoned. *(US Senate Judiciary Committee 1993)*
- Women of all ethnicities are raped: American Indian/Alaska Native women are most likely to report a rape and Asian/Pacific Islander the least likely. *(National Institute of Justice 1998)*

I'm Back! 163

Sophia

- Reported rape victimization by race is as follows: 34% of American Indian/Alaska Native; 24% women of mixed race; 19% of African American women; 18% of white women; 8% of Asian/Pacific Islander women. *(Tjaden and Thoennes, National Institute of Justice 1998)*

- 80-90% of rapes against women (except for American Indian women) are committed by someone of the same racial background as the victim. *(US Dept. of Justice 1994)*

- American Indian victims of rape reported the offender as either white or black in 90% of reports. *(Department of Justice 1997)*

- In a 1999 longitudinal study of 3,000 women, researchers found women who had been victimized before were seven times more likely to be raped again. *(Acierno, Resnick, Kilpatrick, Saunders and Best, Jnl. of Anxiety Disorders 13, 6.)*

- 93% of women and 86% of men who were raped and/or physically assaulted since the age of 18 were assaulted by a male. *(National Violence Against Women Survey, 1998)*

- Among female rape victims, 61% are under age 18. *(American Academy of Pediatrics, 1995)*

- 22% of females raped are under the age of 12 years; 32% are 12-17 years old; 29% 18-24 years old; 17% over 25 years old. 83% of those raped are under the age of 25 years old. *(National Institute of Justice 1998)*

I'm Back!

Sophia

- In a study of 6,000 students at 32 colleges in the US, 1 in 4 women had been the victims of rape or attempted rape. *(Warshaw 1994)*

- 13% of college women indicated they had been forced to have sex in a dating situation. *(Johnson and Sigler, Jnl. of Interpersonal Violence, 2000)*

- In a study of 6,000 students at 32 colleges in the US, 42% of rape victims told no-one and only 5% reported it to the police. *(Warshaw 1994)*

- 1 in 12 male students surveyed had committed acts that met the legal definition of rape or attempted rape. *(Warshaw, Robin 1994 "I Never Called It Rape")*

- In a survey of college males who committed rape, 84% said what they did was definitely not rape. *(Warshaw, Robin 1994 "I Never Called It Rape")*

- A study of 477 male students, mostly 1st and 2nd year students, found 56% reported instances of non-assault coercion to obtain sex. Examples included: threatening to end a relationship; falsely professing love; telling lies to render her more sexually receptive. *(Boeringer 1996, Violence Against Women:5)*

- Women with disabilities are raped and abused at twice the rate of the general population. *(Sobsey 1994)*

I'm Back!

Sophia

- Of the 22 substances used in drug facilitated rape, alcohol is the most common finding in investigations. *(Jnl. of Forensic Sciences 1999)*

- According to the First National Survey of Transgender Violence, 13.7% of 402 persons reported being a victim of rape or attempted rape. *(Gender PAC 1997)*

- A 1991 study of college gay, lesbian and bisexual students found that 18% had been victims of rape and 12% victims of attempted rape. *(Jnl. Of College Student Development)*

- 15% of women who lived with a man as a couple reported being raped/assaulted or stalked by a male cohabitant. *(1999 Centers for Disease Control and Prevention)*

- 6 out of 10 rapes are reported by victims where the incidents have occurred in their own home or home of a friend, relative or neighbor. *(US Dept. of Justice 1997)*

- Sexual assault is reported by 33-46% of women who are being physically assaulted by their husbands. *(AMA 1995)*

*Gathered from UCSC Rape Prevention Statistics website: http://www2.ucsc.edu/rape-prevention/statistics.html

I'm Back!

Sophia

YOU CAN DO IT!

Sophia

YOU are somebody, you are worth being loved by a true man or woman of God, and you are beautiful no matter what people say. God made you, and no one can compete with that. He's always with you even when you don't feel His presence. Just press; just cry; just believe that God can and will work it out for you. Praise Him in the good and the bad. Praise Him when you're happy and sad. Praise Him when you don't feel like it. Praise Him down to your last dime. Praise Him because God's in control!

I'm Back!

Sophia

Phil. 4:13

I can do all things through Christ which strentheneth me.

I pray that this small excerpt from my life will help you realize that despite your circumstances and the obstacles, you are better than anything Satan can throw your way or that God can allow you to go through. I'm a living witness that when others count you out, God counts you in. Despite the abuse, despite the lies, I believed I would be more than a statistic. Spread out in book form, my story may not seem as harsh as it actually was in reality; however, in retrospect the ugly things that happened to me are unimaginable: but the

Sophia

positive things that I accomplished are also worthy to be reported, as well.

Brief Timeline

Age	Report
• 9 to 11	Molested continuously by father
• 13 to 15	Raped three times
• 15	Moved out of Mother's with newborn son
• 16	Occupied my first apartment
• 17	Graduated Waco High School
• 20	Purchased first home in Springfield, MA
• 21	Started own business
• 22	Graduated Cum Laude, BSBA from AIC
• 23	Graduated w/ 3.7 - MBA from AIC
• 24	Married
• 27	Divorced and Headed Toward Recovery
• 29	Working with MLK III, L. Tomlinson
• 29	Published 1st of 4 books!

At 29 years old I'm a single mother of three beautiful children and have custody of my younger brother Francois. I'm currently working with my nonprofit Empowerment

I'm Back!

Sophia

Driven by Knowledge Coalition with our motto "Rebuilding Communities One Family at a Time." My business Trustworthy Consulting is growing and continuing to aid non profits and small businesses with the dedicated mission "A Business Designed to give God's people the keys to prosperity (www.trustworthyconsult.com). And here I am still standing. GOD IS AWESOMELY INDESCRIBABLY WONDERFUL!

Sophia

All my days won't be sunshine; however, I know who controls the storm and rain so I can rest assured that troubles won't last always. I encourage you to remember to strive for excellence and settle for nothing less.

Sophia Antwonique Strother

I'm Back!

Sophia

HELPFUL ORGANIZATIONS FOR SURVIVORS AND/OR SURVIVORS' FAMILY AND FRIENDS

RAINN- Rape, Abuse, Incest National Network

www.rainn.org

Take Back the Night

www.takebackthenight.org

Rape Is

www.rapeis.org

National Foundation to Prevent Child Sexual Abuse

www.fbifingerprintcheck.com

National Sexual Violence Resource Center

www.nsvrc.org

National Organization on Male Sexual Victimization

www.malesurvivor.org

IF YOU HAVE BEEN A VICTIM OR KNOW SOMEONE WHO HAS **PLEASE REPORT** IT TO LAW ENFORCEMENT. ONLY 2% OF OFFENDERS ARE PROSECUTED AND ONLY 16% OF SEXUAL ABUSE CRIMES ARE EVEN REPORTED. PLEASE DON'T LIVE AS A VICTIM! LIVE AS A **SURVIVOR**!

I'm Back!

Sophia

TO BOOK SOPHIA FOR MOTIVATIONAL SPEAKING, WORKSHOPS AND/OR BOOK PURCHASE:

Empowerment Driven by Knowledge Coalition

PO Box 273
Waco, Texas 76703
www.trustworthyconsult.com
trustworthy.consulting@yahoo.com
(254) 495-5556 direct

Next Book Coming Soon!

"Chain Reaction"

Why Does He Seem So Familiar?

This book will deal with the question we always ask, "Why do I attract the no-goods and losers?" "Why do I always find myself in unhealthy and emotionally damaging relationships?"

Trust me. I can relate and I'm ready to acknowledge that I personally had to take some responsibility for the cycle that we call "Chain Reaction." So join me in my own personal detailed journey of relationships and find out how to break free from the cycle!

I'm Back!

Sophia

Join me on…

FACEBOOK
Sophia Strother

YOUTUBE
SOPHIASTROTHER

TWITTER
@sophiasback

MYSPACE
sophiasback

I'm Back!

CPSIA information can be obtained
at www.ICGtesting.com
Printed in the USA
LVHW02s1754050718
582799LV00011B/486/P